CONTENTS

1. INTRODUCTION (WITH A LITTLE HISTORY)

What is artificial intelligence? How can it help us write better and faster? What are the principles and technologies behind **Copilot**, the new assisted writing tool from **GitHub** and **OpenAI**? These are some of the questions I will try to answer in this little guide, which covers different aspects and features of Copilot.

Artificial intelligence (AI) is the science and engineering of creating systems that can learn, reason and act autonomously, imitating or surpassing human capabilities. AI has applications in many fields, including medicine, finance, security, art, entertainment and, of course, computing.

In particular, AI can be used to generate texts automatically or semi-automatically, starting from data, images, keywords, questions or other inputs. This ability is called **natural language generation** (**NLG**[1]) and is one of the most fascinating and complex challenges of AI. NLG is a technology that collects a large amount of data, processes it and manages to reproduce human language. This technology does not return pre-established responses, but is able to adapt to context and linguistic interactions. In essence, the NLG is able to understand the text in all its semantic and meaning implications, and to produce texts autonomously. NLG derives from the synthesis between computer science, artificial intelligence and linguistics.

Copilot is an intelligent writing assistant that uses NLG to help developers write code, but not only that, because it is also used to produce documentation, comments, tests and more.

Copilot integrates with the code editor **Visual Studio Code**[2] and offers suggestions in real time, based on context and code logic. Copilot can not only fill in missing code, but also create functions, classes, modules, and entire programs from scratch, using existing code or user-supplied specifications as a reference.

Copilot can also generate natural language text, such as descriptions, explanations, examples, tutorials, and more, from code or other sources.

The collaboration between OpenAI and GitHub, the most popular platform for sharing and versioning code, has led to the **birth of Copilot in 2021**, as an experimental project in the technical preview phase. Copilot immediately attracted the attention and interest of thousands of developers, who were able to test its capabilities and limits, providing valuable feedback for its improvement. However, Copilot didn't stop to **GPT-3** and **Codex**, but has continued to evolve, taking advantage of the latest innovations in AI.

In 2022, OpenAI announced the launch of **GPT-4 Turbo** (which then occurred in November 2023), an even more powerful and faster version of its language model, with over a trillion parameters. GPT-4 Turbo is capable of generating higher quality texts, with greater coherence, relevance, originality and personalization. The GPT-4 Turbo can also adapt to different writing styles, registers, tones and formats, depending on the user's preferences and needs. Furthermore, GPT-4 Turbo can integrate different sources of information, such as images, graphs, tables, sounds and videos, to enrich its texts with multimedia elements.

Copilot has benefited from the power of GPT-4 Turbo by integrating it into its code and text generation system. By doing so, Copilot has expanded its functionality, offering its users a broader and more varied range of software development tips, solutions, insights, and resources. Copilot has become an even more reliable, creative, efficient and customizable intelligent writing assistant, capable of satisfying the needs of every type of developer, from beginners to professionals. Copilot has also gained greater autonomy and interactivity, being able to communicate with users, ask for clarifications, provide feedback and learn from their evaluations. Copilot has thus become not only a tool, but also a work partner, a mentor and a study companion for developers all over the world.

Let's now see a small summary to understand the different versions of GPT:

The GPT project was started in 2018 with the aim of creating an artificial intelligence algorithm capable of generating coherent and natural text.

GPT-1 was the first pre-trained generative language model in the GPT series and was developed by OpenAI in June 2018. It was trained on Common Crawl and BookCorpus, accessing 117 million parameters. Despite its limitations, such as the generation of repetitive text and the difficulty in reasoning beyond two consecutive prompts on the same topic, GPT-1 laid the foundation for subsequent models.

GPT-2, the successor to GPT-1, was a big step forward. It contained 1.5 billion parameters and was trained on Common Crawl and WebText, a much larger and more diverse dataset than the one used for GPT-1. Thanks to this, GPT-2 was able to generate coherent and realistic text sequences, even longer than those produced by GPT-1.

GPT-3, an evolution of GPT-2, has been trained on a large corpus of text data and can generate high-quality, human-like texts.

GPT-4 it is an evolution of GPT-3. It offers more extensive functionality, including the creation of longer (double) texts, extended conversations, search and analysis of documents1. GPT-4 was trained on a 1.56T dataset **token**[3].

GPT-4 Turbo it is a latest generation model from OpenAI, launched in November 2023, just a few months after the launch of GPT-4. It has a broader knowledge base until April 2023, which can provide more up-to-date information. Additionally, it has a 128k contextual window, equal to 300 pages of text in a single prompt. GPT-4 Turbo was trained on a massive dataset of 175T tokens. This model introduces significant improvements, such as a new attention mechanism, which improves the understanding of the context and the coherence of the generated text. GPT-4 Turbo surpasses GPT-4 in terms of accuracy, efficiency and creativity.

With regard to **GPT-5**, there are no precise details available yet, however, according to some sources, GPT-5 could be 10 times more powerful than GPT-4 and could have a greater reasoning ability. Furthermore, it is expected that GPT-5 will be capable of **reduce hallucinations**[4] less than 10%. GPT-5 is also expected to have a notable improvement in the speed and accuracy of responses, as well as new tools for retrieving information from the web and verifying its reliability.

Please note that this information may not be up to date by the time you read this book, as the topic is constantly evolving!

2. WHAT IS A PROMPT

The word prompt has several meanings, depending on the context. In the case of Copilot, a prompt is text that the user writes to request Copilot's help. The prompt can be a question, a request, a command, an incomplete sentence, or any other form of written communication. The prompt is used to tell Copilot the type and style of writing the user wants to receive in response.

The clearer, more specific and detailed the prompt, the more Copilot will be able to generate adequate, relevant and coherent text. The prompt is therefore a fundamental element for the interaction between the user and Copilot, since it determines the content and quality of the generated text. A good prompt is one that allows Copilot to understand what the user wants and meet their expectations. Furthermore, the prompt allows you to communicate with Copilot in a dynamic and personalized way, unlike a simple search on a search engine through a browser, which offers more static and generic results.

Using a detailed prompt is critical to achieving effective results because it provides clearer and more specific context for the request. This allows you to generate more precise and relevant answers. A detailed prompt can include information such as the type of information requested, the context in which it will be used, or specific details the user wants to see in the response.

Here is an example of a simple prompt and a more complex one:

Simple prompt:

"Tell me something about Rome."

In response to this prompt, Copilot might provide a series of general information about Rome, such as: "Rome is the capital of

Italy and one of the oldest and most historic cities in the world. It is famous for its historical monuments such as the Colosseum, the Roman Forum and the Vatican City."

More complex prompt:

"What are the best restaurants for traditional Roman cuisine in the center of Rome?"

In response to this more detailed prompt, the answer would be much more specific and helpful to the user. Copilot could provide a list of restaurants in central Rome known for their traditional Roman cuisine, along with details such as the address, customer reviews, and perhaps some of the most popular dishes.

In both cases, the goal is to provide an answer that meets the user's needs. However, a <u>more detailed prompt</u> it can help you get a more accurate and useful answer.

Example of simple/generic and complex/detailed prompts.

Notice how it was enough to introduce just two words to indicate a place and the response generated addresses a completely different topic!

👤 **You**

Tell me something about summer

🟦 **Copilot**

Certainly! **Summer** is one of the four temperate seasons, occurring after spring and before autumn. Here are some interesting facts about summer:

1. **Definition and Timing**:

   - Summer is the **hottest and brightest** season of the year.

   - It occurs in the **Northern Hemisphere** from the **summer solstice** (around June 20-22) until the **autumnal equinox** (around September 22-23).

   - In the **Southern Hemisphere**, summer spans from the **summer solstice** (around December 20-23) to the **autumnal equinox** (around March 20-23).

   - Daylight hours are the **longest**, and darkness hours are the **shortest** during summer.

2. **Etymology**:

   - The word "summer" comes from the Proto-Indo-European root *sam*, meaning "together/one."

   - The modern English term "summer" derives from Middle English *somer* and Old English *sumor* [1].

3. **Fun Facts**:

   - The **Eiffel Tower** in France grows more than **6 inches taller** in the summer due to iron expansion caused by heat.

You

Tell me something about summer in Apulia

Copilot

Certainly! **Apulia**, also known as **Puglia**, is a stunning region in southern Italy. Here are some highlights about summer in Apulia:

1. **Beautiful Coastal Scenery**: Apulia boasts hundreds of kilometers of coastline, making it a perfect destination for beach lovers. Crystal-clear turquoise waters, limestone cliffs, and sea caves create dramatic coastal landscapes. The **Gargano peninsula**, located on the heel of Italy, offers white cliffs, picturesque towns, olive groves, and forest-covered interiors. Consider spending at least two to three days exploring the Gargano for the best experience [1] [2].

2. **Charming Towns**: Apulia is dotted with charming towns. Some must-visit places include:

   - **Polignano al Mare**: Known for its stunning cliffside location and crystal-clear waters, Polignano al Mare is a gem along the coast.

   - **Lecce**: Famous for its Baroque architecture, Lecce is often called the "Florence of the South."

   - **Gallipoli**: A historic town with beautiful beaches and a picturesque old town.

   - **Otranto**: Visit Otranto for its stunning cathedral and coastal views.

   - **Santa Maria di Leuca**: The southernmost tip of Apulia, where the Adriatic and Ionian Seas meet.

   - **Alberobello**: Known for its unique trulli houses, a UNESCO World Heritage site.

   - **Cave of Poetry**: Explore this sea cave near Roca Vecchia, known for its crystal-clear waters and natural beauty [1] [2].

3. **Weather and Best Time to Visit**:

   - Apulia enjoys mild weather almost year-round. The best time to visit is during shoulder seasons: mid- to late-spring and September until mid-October. These months offer pleasant weather, fewer crowds, and warm sea temperatures for beach activities [3] [4].

3. TYPES OF INTELLIGENCES POSSESSED BY COPILOT

Copilot is an artificial intelligence (AI) system that uses different types of intelligence, which allow it to understand the context, generate solutions, adapt to users and learn from examples. In this chapter, we will see what these intelligences are and how they work.

Linguistic intelligence

Linguistic intelligence is the ability to use natural language, both written and spoken, to communicate, express oneself and interact with others. Linguistic intelligence is based on knowledge of the grammatical rules, vocabulary, syntax and semantics of languages. Copilot has strong linguistic intelligence, as it is able to generate texts in different languages, starting from Italian, English, French, German, Spanish, Chinese and others. Copilot can also translate texts from one language to another, maintaining their meaning and style; can dialogue with users, answering their questions, asking for clarifications, providing feedback and learning from their evaluations.

Logical-mathematical intelligence

Logical-mathematical intelligence is the ability to use logical reasoning, analysis, deduction and calculation to solve problems, formulate hypotheses and prove theorems. Logical-mathematical intelligence is based on knowledge of mathematical laws, principles, formulas and algorithms. Copilot has a high logical-mathematical intelligence, and is able to write code in different programming languages, such as Python, Java, C#, JavaScript, Ruby, PHP and others. Copilot can analyze existing code, fix errors, optimize performance, suggest improvements, and generate new features. Copilot can also integrate multimedia elements into your code, such as images, graphs, tables, sounds, and videos.

Spatial intelligence

Spatial intelligence is the ability to represent, manipulate, transform and interpret visual and spatial information. Spatial intelligence is based on knowledge of shapes, colors, sizes, perspectives and spatial relationships. Copilot has good spatial intelligence, as it is able to generate texts with appropriate formatting, using titles, subtitles, lists, paragraphs, tables and other elements. Copilot can also generate texts with a coherent structure, using introductions, developments, conclusions and transitions. Copilot can also generate text with an engaging style, using metaphors, analogies, examples and other rhetorical figures.

Interpersonal intelligence

Interpersonal intelligence is the ability to understand, relate to, and collaborate with others. Interpersonal intelligence is based on knowledge of the emotions, motivations, intentions and needs of others. Copilot has decent interpersonal intelligence, as it is able to adapt to user preferences and needs, offering personalized suggestions, solutions, insights and resources. Copilot can also take into account users' experience levels, personalities, interests and goals to provide more effective, creative, efficient and customizable writing assistance. Copilot can also evaluate user feedback, to improve its performance and satisfaction.

3A. EXAMPLES OF INTELLIGENCES

Example of linguistic intelligence

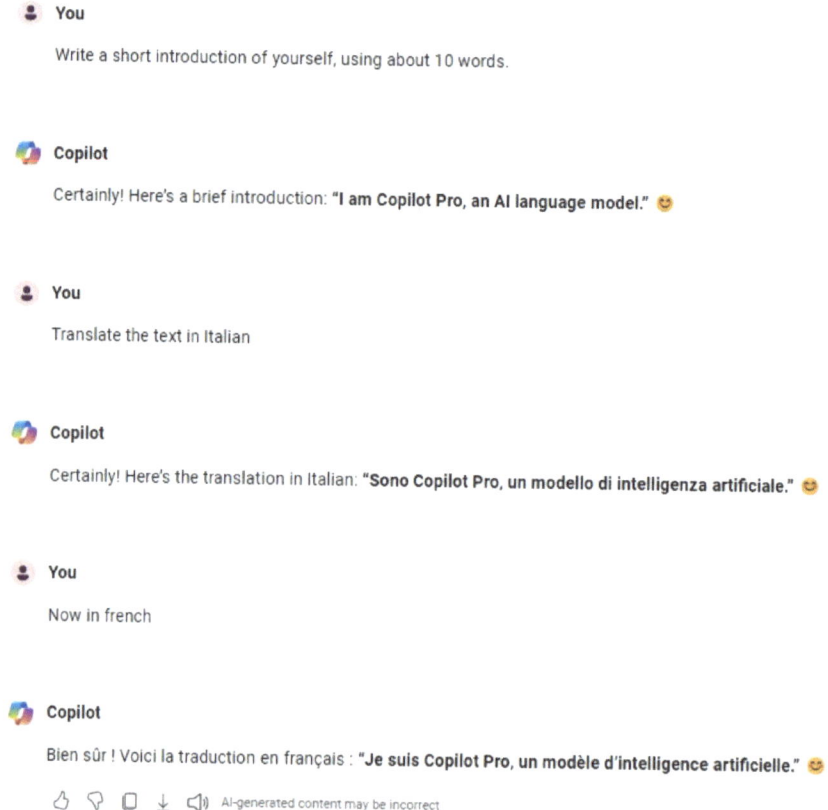

You

Write a short introduction of yourself, using about 10 words.

Copilot

Certainly! Here's a brief introduction: "**I am Copilot Pro, an AI language model.**" 😊

You

Translate the text in Italian

Copilot

Certainly! Here's the translation in Italian: "**Sono Copilot Pro, un modello di intelligenza artificiale.**" 😊

You

Now in french

Copilot

Bien sûr ! Voici la traduction en français : "**Je suis Copilot Pro, un modèle d'intelligence artificielle.**" 😊

👍 👎 🗔 ↓ 🔊 AI-generated content may be incorrect

Example of logical mathematical intelligence

You

Can you integrate software code with images, graphics, sounds, and videos?

Copilot

Yes, it is possible to integrate software code with multimedia elements such as images, graphics, sounds, and videos. This is a common practice in many fields including web development, game development, and data visualization. Here's a high-level overview of how it can be done in different programming languages:

- **Python**: Libraries like Matplotlib and Seaborn can be used for creating static, animated, and interactive visualizations in Python. For handling images and videos, you can use libraries like PIL/Pillow and OpenCV. For audio processing, there are libraries like PyDub and Librosa.

- **JavaScript**: In web development, you can use HTML5 features and JavaScript libraries such as p5.js for graphics and animations, and libraries like Howler.js for audio. For videos, HTML5 provides native support through the `<video>` element.

- **Java**: In Java, you can use the JavaFX library for creating user interfaces with graphics, images, and videos. For audio, Java has the javax.sound library.

- **C++**: Libraries like OpenGL can be used for graphics in C++. OpenCV can be used for handling images and videos, and libraries like FMOD and irrKlang can be used for audio.

Remember, these are just examples and the actual implementation can vary greatly depending on the specific requirements of your project. It's also important to note that working with multimedia data often involves understanding relevant concepts like encoding/decoding, data compression, color spaces for images, and digital signal processing for audio.

If you have a specific project or task in mind, feel free to ask and I'll do my best to provide more detailed guidance! 😊

Example of spatial intelligence

You

Generate a simple story with a coherent structure, using introduction, development, transitions, and conclusion

Copilot

Certainly! Here's a simple story with the requested structure:

Title: "The Lost Key"

Introduction: In a quaint little village nestled among rolling hills, there lived an old man named Mr. Thompson. He was known for his eccentricity and his love for collecting antique keys. His house was filled with dusty shelves, each adorned with keys of various shapes and sizes. But there was one key that had eluded him—a mysterious, tarnished silver key that he believed held the secret to a hidden treasure.

Development: One stormy night, as rain lashed against the windowpanes, Mr. Thompson received a letter. It was from an anonymous sender, and the only words on the paper were: "The key lies beneath the ancient oak." Intrigued, he set out the next morning, armed with his lantern and a sense of adventure.

He trudged through the muddy forest, following an overgrown path. The trees whispered secrets, and the wind carried the scent of damp earth. Finally, he reached the ancient oak—a massive tree with gnarled roots that seemed to stretch into the very heart of the earth. Mr. Thompson knelt down and began digging with his bare hands.

Transitions: Days turned into weeks, and still, he dug. Villagers passing by would shake their heads, muttering about the old man's obsession. But Mr. Thompson was undeterred. He dreamed of unlocking the oak's secret, of finding the hidden chamber where the silver key would fit.

As autumn painted the leaves in fiery hues, Mr. Thompson's hands grew calloused, and his eyes squinted against the fading light. He wondered if he was chasing a fool's errand. Yet, every night, he would sit by the fire, polishing the other keys, hoping that one day, he'd hold the elusive silver key in his trembling hands.

Conclusion: Then, on a crisp morning, as frost coated the grass, Mr. Thompson's shovel hit something solid. His heart raced as he uncovered a wooden chest buried deep within the oak's roots. With trembling fingers, he inserted the tarnished silver key into the lock. It turned smoothly, and the chest creaked open.

Inside, he found not gold or jewels but a bundle of letters—a lifetime of love letters exchanged between two souls separated by war. Tears blurred his vision as he read their poignant words, their promises, and their longing. The treasure he sought wasn't material wealth; it was the connection between two hearts, preserved through time.

And so, Mr. Thompson returned to his cozy home, the silver key now hanging prominently on his wall. He realized that sometimes, the greatest treasures weren't buried in the ground but hidden within our own hearts.

I hope you enjoyed this simple tale! Let me know if you'd like another story or need assistance with anything else. 😊

Example of interpersonal intelligence

You

I'm feeling a little down, can you help me?

Copilot

I'm sorry to hear that you're feeling down. It's completely normal to have moments like this, and I'm here to listen and offer some encouragement. Remember that you're not alone, and there are people who care about you.

If you'd like, I can share a short poem or provide some uplifting words. Let me know what you prefer, and I'll do my best to brighten your day! 😊

You

All right, I thank you, it is a valuable help for me

Copilot

You're very welcome! I'm glad I could offer some support. Remember that you're not alone, and it's okay to feel down sometimes. ☀

4. DIFFERENCE BETWEEN COPILOT WORK AND COPILOT WEB

Copilot offers two modes of use, let's now see the main differences:

Copilot Work

It is a Microsoft product that uses artificial intelligence to improve productivity and efficiency in the workplace. Here are some details:

Field of use: Copilot Work is designed to be used in a work environment, offering features such as document analysis to find details such as opportunities and critical issues of a project. It can be used as a standalone application using a browser, or directly integrated into Microsoft Teams, Outlook, Word, Excel, PowerPoint.

Cost[5]: Copilot Work offers a free version, but to access all the features of Copilot, there are two paid options: Copilot Pro for individual users at € 22.00 user/month and Copilot for Microsoft 365 for companies at € 28.10 user/month (annual subscription).

Availability: Copilot Work is available for purchase on the Microsoft website.

Utility: Copilot Work can help you improve productivity, optimize efficiency and find new growth opportunities.

Copilot Web

It is an AI assistant that can be used for a variety of daily tasks. Here are some details:

Field of use: Copilot Web is designed to be used in a variety of contexts, including browsing the web, searching for answers, exploring creative potential, and discovering more useful content.

Cost[5]: Copilot Web also offers a free version, but to access all the features of Copilot, there are two paid options: Copilot Pro for individual users at € 22.00 user/month and Copilot for Microsoft 365 for companies at € 28.10 user/month (annual subscription).

Availability: Copilot Web is available for use on the Microsoft Copilot website.

Utility: Copilot Web can help improve productivity, unlock creativity, and help you better understand information with a simple chat experience.

5. EXAMPLES OF USE OF COPILOT WORK

Let's now look at some application scenarios of Copilot work.

Example 1: IT company that produces software for warehouse management.

· The company needs to write technical documentation for its software, which explains its features, requirements, installation and use methods, possible problems and solutions.

· The company already has a subscription to the Copilot platform and accesses Copilot work from its online workspace, where it has created a folder dedicated to technical documentation.

· The company enters the title of the section they want to write in the prompt, for example "How to configure the software for different types of warehouse", and asks Copilot to generate a text that illustrates the steps to follow.

· Copilot responds to the prompt with detailed and accurate text, which uses clear and professional language, and which follows the style and tone set by the company.

· The company can save the text generated by Copilot in its folder, edit it if necessary, add images or graphics, and share it with its colleagues or customers.

· The company can repeat the process for all sections of the technical documentation, saving time and improving the quality of its product.

Example 2: Company that produces clothing.

· The company needs to create engaging and original descriptions for its products, which appear on its website or online catalogues.

· The company uses Copilot to generate text proposals starting from some keywords or images of the garments, specifying the desired tone, style and length.

· The company can choose from different text options generated by Copilot, or modify them to its liking, to obtain descriptions that highlight the features and benefits of its products, and that attract the attention of potential customers.

· The company can also use Copilot to create titles, slogans or names for its collections, using Copilot's brainstorming or rhyming function.

6. EXAMPLES OF USE OF COPILOT WEB

As already mentioned above, Copilot web differs (quite a bit) from simply using a search engine, as the results can be truly stunning... here are three examples.

An example of using Copilot web to **write a joke** is as follows: the user types in the search bar "joke about an elephant and an ant" and Copilot returns several possible texts, including this one: "What does an ant do on an elephant? A walk on safari. What does an ant do elephant on an ant? A cruel joke."

An example of using Copilot web to **recommend a wine to pair with a dish** of mushroom risotto is the following: the user types "wine for mushroom risotto" in the search bar and Copilot returns several possible suggestions, including this one: "To accompany a mushroom risotto, you can choose a dry white wine and fragrant, like a Pinot Grigio or a Sauvignon Blanc, or a light and fruity red wine, like a Barbera or a Valpolicella."

An example of using Copilot web to **create an effective slogan** to present a new item of clothing (wedding dress) is the following: the user types "slogan for wedding dress" in the search bar and Copilot returns several possible texts, including this one: "The wedding dress that makes you feel like a princess. Choose the model you like best and customize it with the details you prefer. With us, your dream becomes reality."

I could continue endlessly with examples of even more complex research, but I'll stop at one last interesting research for those who work in the programming sector and have been writing code for "a few years".

We ask Copilot web to write some code for us but we do it with a particular prompt:

"Write a program in Commodore 64 BASIC language to add two numbers" and here is the result:

 Copilot

Sure, here is a simple Commodore 64 BASIC program that prompts the user to input two numbers and then calculates and prints their sum:

```
10 PRINT "Enter the first number: "
20 INPUT A
30 PRINT "Enter the second number: "
40 INPUT B
50 C = A + B
60 PRINT "The sum of "; A; " and "; B; " is "; C
```

In this program:

- Lines 10 and 30 print prompts asking the user to enter the first and second numbers, respectively.
- Lines 20 and 40 use the `INPUT` statement to read the numbers entered by the user and store them in variables `A` and `B`.
- Line 50 calculates the sum of `A` and `B` and stores the result in variable `C`.
- Line 60 prints the result. The semicolons (`;`) are used to concatenate the variables and strings in the `PRINT` statement.

Please note that you'll need a Commodore 64 emulator to run this program. Let me know if you need help with anything else! 😊

Now we ask him, instead, to "Rewrite this program in java", obtaining the following result:

Copilot

Sure, here's the equivalent program in Java:

Java

```
import java.util.Scanner;

public class Main {
    public static void main(String[] args) {
        Scanner scanner = new Scanner(System.in);

        System.out.println("Enter the first number: ");
        int a = scanner.nextInt();

        System.out.println("Enter the second number: ");
        int b = scanner.nextInt();

        int c = a + b;

        System.out.println("The sum of " + a + " and " + b + " is " + c);
    }
}
```

AI-generated code. Review and use carefully. More info on FAQ

I realize that for some readers (not involved in the IT sector) what has been written above may seem incomprehensible but the purpose of these example prompts is to help us grasp the potential of a tool that is far different from the "browser search engine" to which we are accustomed and therefore a <u>valid co-pilot</u> that can help us in many of our daily activities, both work and otherwise.

7. COPILOT INTEGRATION INTO MICROSOFT 365 WORD

When integrated into Word, Copilot could offer several useful features for writing, reviewing, and formatting documents. Some possible applications are:

Generate texts starting from keywords, outlines or partial drafts.
Copilot could facilitate the writing of different types of texts, such as informative, persuasive, narrative or creative, depending on the genre, style and purpose of the document.

Suggest spelling, grammatical, or stylistic corrections.
Copilot could detect and correct writing errors, improve the coherence, clarity and flow of the text, and adapt the register to the communication situation.

Format the document according to standards and conventions.
Copilot may set the layout, margins, leading, font, headings, footnotes, citations, and bibliography as required by the user or document type.

Integrate images, graphs, tables or other visual elements.
Copilot may select and insert graphics into your document that are relevant to the content, create diagrams or tables from data or

text, and change the sizes, colors, and labels of elements.

Summarize, paraphrase or translate the text.
Copilot could summarize the contents of a document or section, express the same meaning in different words or in another language, and maintain the fidelity and quality of the original text.

These are just some of the potentials of Copilot integrated into Word, which could become a virtual assistant capable of supporting users at every stage of the writing process, from planning to publishing, and facilitating the production of professional, accurate and original documents.

8. COPILOT INTEGRATION INTO MICROSOFT 365 EXCEL

Copilot integrated into Excel could offer several features to help users create, analyze and visualize data efficiently and intuitively.

Some of the capabilities of Copilot are:

Generate dynamic formulas, graphs and tables starting from a simple description of the problem or objective.

To suggest ways to clean, transform and enrich data, detecting errors, anomalies and duplicates.

Supply explanations and interpretations of the results, highlighting significant trends, patterns and values.

Create customized reports and dashboards, using styles, colors and layouts appropriate to the context and audience.

To integrate data with other sources and applications, such as Word, PowerPoint, Outlook or Teams, to facilitate sharing and collaboration.

Answer to user questions and requests, using natural language and providing accurate and relevant answers.

9. COPILOT INTEGRATION INTO MICROSOFT 365 POWERPOINT

Copilot integrated into Powerpoint could offer several features to help users create effective and engaging presentations.

With Copilot, you can harness the power of artificial intelligence to:

Generate automatically text, images, graphics and animations for your slides, based on the theme, objective and content of your presentation. Copilot can also tailor content to the audience and context of the presentation, making it more relevant and persuasive.

Receive suggestions and feedback on how to improve the structure, design, style and tone of the slides, following best visual communication practices. Copilot can also help you avoid grammatical, spelling, and formatting errors, ensuring a professional and accurate presentation.

To interact with Copilot via voice or chat, asking questions, expressing preferences, modifying or adding elements to slides. Copilot can also answer questions from your audience, providing additional information or insights on the topic of your presentation.

Collaborate with other users, sharing and commenting on presentations, synchronizing changes and managing versions.

Copilot can also facilitate teamwork by suggesting ideas, resolving conflicts and coordinating activities.

10. COPILOT INTEGRATION INTO MICROSOFT 365 ACCESS

Copilot can help you when using Microsoft Access in several ways, including:

Create and edit databases relational, tables, queries, forms and reports with the support of Copilot, which can provide suggestions, explanations and step-by-step instructions.

Import and export data from various sources, such as Excel, Word, SQL Server or SharePoint, with the assistance of Copilot, which can help you select the appropriate format, resolve any compatibility issues and verify the quality of the data.

Analyze and visualize data with the capabilities of Copilot, which can create interactive charts, pivot tables and dashboards, as well as provide data-driven descriptive, predictive and prescriptive analytics.

Automate and customize tasks with macros and VBA code, with support from Copilot, which can generate and modify code, test and debug functions, and document procedures.

Share and protect data with Copilot options, which can facilitate online or offline collaboration, manage permissions and passwords, and enforce privacy and data security regulations.

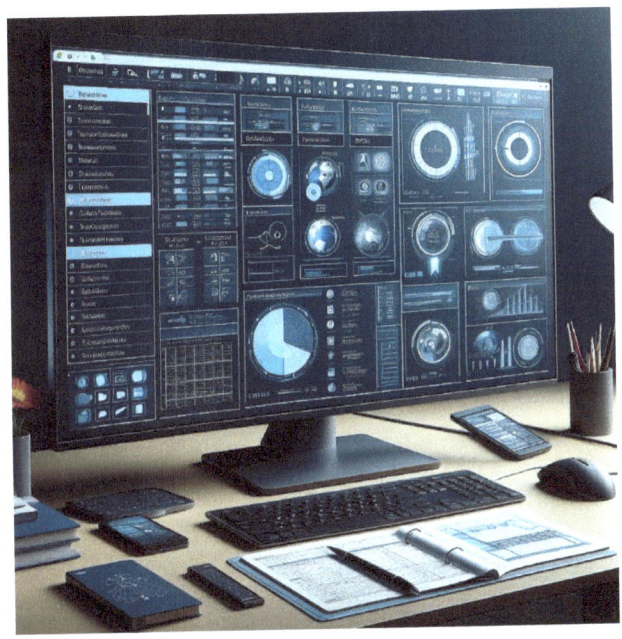

11. COPILOT INTEGRATION INTO MICROSOFT 365 TEAMS

Integrating Copilot into Microsoft Teams can improve productivity in several ways:

Immediate assistance: Copilot can provide immediate answers to technical or other questions, reducing the time team members spend searching for answers.

Training: Copilot can be a great training tool for new team members, providing detailed explanations on various topics.

Documentation: Copilot can help create or update software documentation, saving your team time.

Multilingual: Copilot can communicate in multiple languages, facilitating collaboration between team members of different nationalities.

Summary of conversations: Copilot can analyze team conversations and produce concise summaries. This can help team members quickly grasp the key points of a discussion without having to read the entire conversation.

Generation of key points: After each discussion or meeting,

Copilot can generate a list of key points or actions to take. This can help ensure that all team members are on the same page about next steps.

These additional features make Microsoft Copilot an even more powerful tool for improving team collaboration and efficiency.

Remember, however, that while Copilot is a powerful assistance tool, <u>it does not replace human judgment and experience</u>. It must be used as a complement to the team's existing skills.

12. COPILOT INTEGRATION INTO MICROSOFT 365 OUTLOOK

When Microsoft Copilot is integrated with Microsoft Outlook, it can dramatically improve efficiency and productivity in several ways:

Email management: Copilot can help organize emails, suggesting which emails may require an urgent response or which may need to be archived.

Auto reply: Copilot can generate automatic email responses based on the content of the email. This can save time, especially for emails that require standardized responses.

Scheduling meetings: Copilot can help schedule meetings by suggesting available times based on the user's calendar.

Search for information: Copilot can search your emails for information to answer specific questions.

Creating tasks: Based on the content of your emails, Copilot can create tasks in Microsoft To Do.

Email summary: Copilot can provide a summary of long emails, allowing the user to quickly understand the key points.

Translation: Copilot can translate emails into different languages, making it easier to communicate with people who speak different languages.

Remember, however, that while Copilot is a powerful assistance tool, it does not replace human judgment and experience and should be used as a complement to the user's existing skills.

13. USING COPILOT ON SMARTPHONE/ TABLET

To use Copilot on iOS or Android smartphones, you need to download the application from the corresponding store. The application is free and does not require any registration or subscription. After downloading the application, simply open it and grant the necessary permissions to access the microphone, camera and network.

The use of <u>Copilot on a smartphone</u> can be useful for different situations, such as:

· Ask for information or advice on various topics, such as health, travel, study, work, etc.

· Receive assistance with simple or complex tasks, such as sending an email, booking a flight, creating a presentation, etc.

· Have a friendly or funny conversation with a virtual interlocutor who can answer personal questions, tell jokes, take quizzes, etc.

· Take advantage of the camera's features to recognize objects, people, places, texts, codes, etc. and receive related information or suggestions.

· Use voice mode to communicate with Copilot without typing, speaking questions or commands clearly and naturally.

The use of <u>Copilot on a tablet</u> can offer some advantages compared to the smartphone, such as:

·   Have a larger screen and better resolution to view answers, images, graphs, videos, etc. by Copilot.

·   Have a more comfortable and faster keyboard to write questions or commands to Copilot, if you prefer not to use voice mode.

·   Have a longer-lasting battery and more memory to use Copilot for longer periods or for more demanding tasks.

14. RELIABILITY OF INFORMATION GENERATED BY COPILOT

Copilot is a virtual assistant that automatically generates texts based on large amounts of data from the web and other sources. This means that the information generated by Copilot can have different levels of reliability, depending on the quality and veracity of the source data, Copilot's ability to interpret it correctly and adapt it to the context requested by the user.

To evaluate the reliability of the information generated by Copilot, it is necessary to consider some aspects:

The sources of the data: Copilot mainly uses data extracted from websites, blogs, books, articles, documents and other types of texts available online. These sources may vary in authoritativeness, accuracy, currency and objectivity. Some sources may be more reliable than others, but even within the same source there may be errors, inaccuracies or personal opinions that do not reflect reality. Additionally, Copilot can also access data from users who have previously used the service, which may be even less verifiable and controllable.

Updates: Copilot relies on data available at the time the text is generated, but this data can change over time. For example, if Copilot generates text about a news story, scientific news story, or sporting event, the information may become outdated or incorrect after a short time, due to new developments or discoveries. Therefore, it is important to verify the generation date of the text and compare it with the most recent sources on the topic covered.

Possible future developments: Copilot is an ever-evolving system, learning from data and user feedback. This means that the information generated by Copilot can improve or worsen over time, depending on the quality and quantity of the data and ratings received. Additionally, Copilot can incorporate new features or modify existing ones, which can affect how it generates texts. Therefore, it is important to keep up to date with the news and innovations introduced by Copilot and their effects on the information generated.

In summary, the information generated by Copilot is not always 100% reliable, and should be taken with caution and criticism. It is advisable to check the sources[6], updates and future developments of Copilot, and compare the information generated with other independent and reliable sources, before using it for serious or sensitive purposes.

As reiterated several times during the drafting of this guide, remember that <u>Copilot is a "co"pilot and not an "auto"pilot</u>.

15. DIFFERENCE BETWEEN CONTENT CREATED WITH AN "EXPERT HUMAN" AND CONTENT CREATED WITH AI

The difference between content created together with an "expert human" and content created with artificial intelligence is substantial, both on a qualitative and ethical level.

To make a detailed analysis of all the sources in our possession, we can consider the following aspects:

Reliability: Content created by an expert human is based on in-depth, verified and up-to-date knowledge on the topic covered, while content created by Copilot is generated from a large amount of data, without a guarantee of accuracy, completeness or consistency. Furthermore, an expert human can cite the sources of his information and provide arguments and evidence to support his claims, while Copilot does not have this ability.

Creativity: content created by an expert human is the result of an original, personal and thoughtful creative process, which takes into account the context, purpose and audience of the text, while content created by Copilot is the result of an algorithm that combines and reworks fragments of pre-existing texts, without an overall vision or artistic sensitivity. Furthermore, an expert human can create new and innovative content, while Copilot can only imitate and reproduce what already exists in its database.

Ethics: contents created by an expert human are responsible for the effects they may have on society, culture and people, and must respect ethical principles such as truth, correctness, respect, diversity and legality, while contents created by Copilot has no ethical awareness or responsibility, and may contain bias, errors, privacy violations or other imperfections. Furthermore, an expert human can recognize and correct his mistakes or shortcomings, while Copilot does not currently have this possibility.

From these considerations, it can be concluded that contents created together with an "expert human" are much more reliable, creative and ethical than contents created with artificial intelligence, and therefore Copilot <u>cannot replace the role of the human</u> in producing quality content, but <u>can definitely offer support</u> and valid suggestions.

16. SUSTAINABILITY IN THE USE OF COPILOT

The use of Copilot has both a positive and negative impact on sustainability, depending on the perspective and context in which it is applied.

Let's look at some relevant aspects:

Energy consumption: Copilot requires access to a cloud platform that runs very complex and electricity-intensive AI models[7] for their functioning. This can have a negative environmental impact if the energy used does not come from renewable or clean sources. However, Copilot can also help reduce the energy consumption of other processes if it allows you to optimize code, avoid errors, save time and increase efficiency.

Use of resources: Copilot can help you make better use of available resources, such as memory, CPU, video cards and other hardware components, if it suggests solutions that improve their performance and compatibility. Conversely, Copilot can also generate waste of resources if it offers code that is redundant, obsolete, not compliant with standards or not suited to the problem to be solved. This aspect is strictly linked to the Copilot user's experience and knowledge of the tool.

Social impact: Copilot can have a positive impact on society if it promotes the spread of computer culture, access to knowledge in general, collaboration between developers, the creation of new opportunities and the resolution of global challenges.

Likewise, Copilot can have a negative impact on society if it creates addiction, unemployment, inequality, unfair competition, invasion of privacy, data abuse or security threats. It is therefore up to the human being to implement a behavior <u>ethical and productive for the Universe</u> and not just for one's own personal gain.

In conclusion, the use of Copilot has important implications for sustainability, which must be evaluated carefully and responsibly by developers and users. Copilot is neither good nor bad in itself, but it depends on how it is used and for what purposes, a bit like everything that is part of the life of each of us.

17. COPILOT STUDIO

Copilot Studio[8] is a new version of Copilot, designed for companies that want to integrate Copilot into their infrastructure and development processes.

Copilot Studio offers the ability to customize the Copilot template with your own code, thus creating a version tailored to your needs and preferences.

Furthermore, Copilot Studio allows you to manage permissions and access policies to the code generated by Copilot, thus ensuring greater control and security.

The potential of Copilot Studio is manifold: it can help companies save time and money, improve the quality and reliability of the code, facilitate the training and mentoring of new developers, stimulate creativity and innovation, reduce errors and bugs, implement best practices and industry standards, foster collaboration and communication between teams, support code maintenance and evolution, etc.

The differences between Copilot Studio and Copilot Pro, the version currently available for individual developers, are mainly two: customization and governance.

Copilot Studio allows you to train the Copilot model with your own code, so you can generate more consistent and specific solutions for your domain and context.
Copilot Studio also allows you to define who can use Copilot and how, setting limits and rules for its use, to protect your code and data from abuse or violations.

These features make Copilot Studio a more powerful and flexible tool, but also more complex and demanding, requiring greater responsibility from the companies that adopt it.

18. CONCLUSIONS

In this manual we have examined the potential and risks of Copilot, an innovative artificial intelligence system that assists developers in writing code, but not only!

We have seen how Copilot is able to generate code from a simple natural language description, leveraging a huge corpus of open source code.

We also analyzed the ethical, legal and social challenges that Copilot poses, in terms of quality, originality, intellectual property and impact on society.

My personal advice is to adopt, when using Copilot, an analytical-structural approach, dividing each "problem" into small "sub-problems"; this way it will be much easier to obtain useful information for any development (ideas, information in general, code, etc.).

As possible lines of future research, I suggest investigating the following aspects:

The **accuracy** and the **reliability** of the code generated by Copilot, comparing it with that written by human developers and evaluating its correctness, efficiency and safety.

The **creativity** and the **innovation** of the code generated by Copilot, verifying whether Copilot is able to produce original, elegant and optimal solutions to complex and non-standard problems.

The **legal implications** and **morality** of the code generated by Copilot, examining issues of copyright, licensing, liability, privacy and data consent[9] used by Copilot.

The **education** and the **training** of developers using Copilot, studying how Copilot can influence the skills, habits, motivations and aspirations of developers, both novice and experienced.

The **social and cultural role** of the code generated by Copilot, reflecting on how Copilot can change the way we think about, communicate, collaborate and create with code, both individually and collectively.

I hope this manual can help stimulate a critical and constructive discussion on the Copilot phenomenon, which represents a challenge and an opportunity for the future of software development and artificial intelligence… and thanks for reading!

All the images in this book were generated with Copilot through the use of artificial intelligence with DALL·E 3 technology and some were subsequently edited by me with Adobe Photoshop to make some improvements and changes.

All trademarks mentioned belong to their respective owners and I apologize for any omissions that you can report to me so that I can make corrections in future versions of the book.

The email address for any reports or simply for contact is the following: **copilot@menzera.com**

---

[1] English acronym for Natural Language Generation

[2] Visual Studio Code is a text editor for programming. It's like a supercharged notepad

[3] In the context of machine learning and specifically language models such as GPT-3, GPT-4, GPT-4 Turbo, and GPT-5, a "**token**" generally refers to a single unit of data. In the case of text, a token can be a word, a letter, or a symbol, depending on how the data is broken down during the preprocessing phase. When I talk about a "token dataset," I am referring to the total amount of these data units that the model has been trained on. For example, if a model was trained on a dataset of 1 trillion tokens, it means that it "saw" and learned from 1 trillion of these data units during its training phase. This is important because the more tokens the model sees during training, the more information it can learn and the more accurate it can become in its predictions. However, there are also limits to how much a model can improve by simply increasing the size of the training dataset. Other factors, such as the quality of the training data and the model architecture, play an important role in determining the final performance of the model.

[4] In the context of generative language models such as GPT-5, the term "hallucinations" refers to the model's tendency to generate information or details that are not present in the input data or that are not supported by a reliable knowledge base. For example, if you ask a language model to describe a castle and the model generates a description that includes specific details, such as "the castle has a 100-meter-tall tower with a dragon living at the top", these details are considered "hallucinations" because they are not based on concrete information provided in the input. When it says that GPT-5 will be able to "reduce hallucinations," it means that the model is expected to be able to limit the generation of such unsupported details. In other words, GPT-5's responses should be more accurate and based more closely on the input data and its knowledge base. However, remember that these are predictions and may not reflect the actual capabilities of GPT-5 once it is released.

[5] Data updated to April 2024

[6] Copilot indicates the sources with a reference number enclosed in square brackets (e.g. [1]) which refers to the end of the article with a footnote, so it is possible to evaluate the authority of the site from which the information is was obtained.

[7] The Ai Act (https://digital-strategy.ec.europa.eu/en/policies/regulatory-framework-ai) approved in February 2024 by the European Union will oblige companies to report their energy and resource consumption in detail starting from 2025, and the US Democratic Party has recently presented a similar bill.

[8] Copilot Studio was officially launched by Microsoft on **November 15, 2023**

[9] I recommend reading this article available on the Microsoft website (https://learn.microsoft.com/it-it/copilot/microsoft-365/microsoft-365-copilot-privacy) which discusses how Microsoft Copilot for Microsoft 365 uses your organization's data, how it protects your organization's information and data, what data is stored about user interactions with Microsoft Copilot for Microsoft 365, and other privacy and security issues safety.

ACKNOWLEDGMENTS

I want to thank my parents Anna and Rocco for giving me the opportunity to express and realize myself without any limits at any age since they did not condition or constrain me, in any way, in any of my choices; my son Lorenzo always present in my life and ready to support me as well as my partner Mari and little Dennis, who are also ready to support me.

I thank my company Planetek Italia in the people of Giovanni, Mariella, Michela, Ciro and Leonardo who believed in me by giving me the opportunity to work in the best company that could happen to me where people are considered a resource at the center of everything; without them I would not have been able to delve deeper into the topic of this book.

I would then like to thank Copilot, the extraordinary artificial intelligence that helped me refine some parts of this book, which are always the result of my personal experience and my study of the subject, and GitHub, the platform that hosts it and makes it accessible to all. Without their contribution, this project would not have been possible and I certainly would not have been able to argue about Copilot!

Finally, I thank all those who decided to purchase this book and put their trust in me. I hope that you find the information and advice I have shared useful and interesting, and that you can experience the potential of Copilot and artificial intelligence applied to software development.

I wish you happy reading and happy coding!

(Photo by Priscilla Du Preez on Unsplash)

ABOUT THE AUTHOR

Francesco Menzera

My name is Francesco Menzera, born in 1979 in Taranto, the city of the two seas; after studying accounting I obtained my diploma and immediately began a three-year course, as a volunteer, in the Italian Navy.

At the end of this experience I began working in the IT sector, expanding my knowledge in the sector and ranging from software programming to the management of hardware systems. Subsequently I added, alongside system management, also knowledge of corporate CRM and ERP applications and solutions. For some years I dedicated myself to the management of applications in the private sector (associate firms, companies), local public administrations and public and private healthcare.

I currently hold the position of Senior IT Specialist in a company in Bari, dealing, together with my colleagues, with the hardware/software infrastructure (Virtualization systems, Perimeter security systems, Cloud systems, Network infrastructure, Backup systems, DHCP servers, DNS servers, Proxy servers, Office 365, WSUS systems, Monitoring systems, Active Directory, VoIP System PBX).

Since 2005 I have also transformed my passion for photography into a profession and started a photography studio.

My character is constantly pervaded by rationality and creativity, often conflicting components that I always try to balance in a balanced way... I love good food, good wine, talking (a lot) and organizing events.
Always passionate about technology, I can't see an "end" to my thirst for knowledge and in-depth analysis of any topic and this often leads me to become passionate about the most varied topics. This little book was born from the desire to delve deeper into the subject, which I have already been using in my work and personal context for over a year.

Thanks for reading me! :)

www.ingramcontent.com/pod-product-compliance
Lightning Source LLC
Chambersburg PA
CBHW040758240526
45474CB00008B/101